Whiskey Jack
A Sisterhood in Verse

Catherine Hamilton Shaw

PublishAmerica
Baltimore

First printing

PublishAmerica has allowed this work to remain exactly as the author intended, verbatim, without editorial input.

Hardcover 978-1-4560-6858-5
Softcover 978-1-4560-6857-8
PUBLISHED BY PUBLISHAMERICA, LLLP
www.publishamerica.com
Baltimore

Printed in the United States of America

Dedication

To those who loved first,
And those who love despite the past.

With Soul's Breath,

Catherine Hamilton Shaw

Table of Contents

LOVE SONG

Huckleberry.. 16

Basics 18

Tonight She's Going to Play 20

What I See.. 22

Shared 24

Say Mine 26

Dream-Delinquent 28

Rite of Passage 30

Caught in Arms 32

First Night 34

He Calls Love 36

Just One.. 38

Signs 40

Breathless 42

Ms. Degree 44

NESTING

Dinner Part 48

Wedding Poem 50

White Dress 52

Bessie 54

Invisible 56

Allegiance 58

That Girl 60

Spent the Night 62

Searching 64

Behind Walls 66

My Closet 68

Dream 70

That Kind of Man 72

THIEVING

Covert.. 76

Sonnet 79

Whisper Love.. 80

Only Love 82

Entangled 84

8 Years.. 86

Promise Easier 88

Some Conversations..............................90

Body 92

Love Her 94

The Joining.. 96

Need You... 98

Melt 100

Full Moon.. 102

Cat and Mouse 104

Nostalgic 106

Stupid Girl... 108

Mourn... 110

Judgment Day 112

Two Options....................................... 114

Plead for Reason 116

Three Times Regression....................... 118

Sheets Down 120

Break-Catch 122

Insatiable Hunger 125

Lady Says Thank You 126

Breakdown 128

All Week 130

Jolting Disgust 132

Adrenaline 134

Take Love 136

Sleeping Over 138

Nightingale to Mockingbird 140

Leaving Type 142

Find Mine 144

The Surrender Box 146

Bleeding Fog 148

Fight Me 150

Admitting Mistakes 152

Silent Speaker 154

Flowers in Bloom 156

Pieces of Us 158

Burned Hope 160

At Least One 162

Tears Tonight 164

FLEDGE

In the Forest 168
Condition of My Heart 170
Confirmations 172
Ballooning 174
At My Door 176
Locked Away 178
Plans 180
Not Just Us 182
Shoes 184
Shell 188
Shh 190
Graceful Goodbye 192
Residual Commitment 194
Shores of Savior 196
For Sale 198

MIGRATION

One 202

Grunge 204

Stuck in Spirals 206

Canvas 208

Words 210

Quiet Strength 212

Stepping Out of Love 214

Sand 216

Dragging 218

Sunset 220

Shattering Truth 222

Returned 224

Days 226

Wild Horses 228

Where You Are 230

Look Around 232

Back to Love 234

Curious Man 236

Sensitive 238

Belonged 240

Questions 242

Locked Within..244
Relinquished Love 246

BROODING

On the Feet of God....................................250

Demanding from Me..............................254

Loving Man...256

The Girl in My Eyes 259

Blurred Flashes 260

On Your Knees..262

Fall Back...266

Based and Built.......................................268

Touched...270

In and Out 272

When You Realize...................................274

Comforter..276

Absent Cause 278

Empathy I..280

Red..282

LOVE SONG

*The strength of a woman
lies within a woman.*

Huckleberry I

Lately filled with
Sadness, anger, disappointment
So help me…
See compassion, loyalty
Know how to lead,
Succeed,
Be everyone's expectation.
So, help me…
Step out from the shadows
Of a first crush,
Loose control,
Breathe deep,
Laugh: whole heart.
Be that for me.

Always protecting,
Always navigating,
Always warning,
Do anything to save me.

Take the time to listen to
Every success and failure
Of the friend falling.

Laugh and cry -
Pull it out -
Crazy but responsible, spoiled but humble,
Naïve but educated, confused but determined -
Be mine.

Huckleberry II

Looking for a fight:
Out to sting the world,
Steal happiness away.
Tread with trepidation;
This isn't vindication.
Jump in puddles of hollowness.

Well, here I am.
She's got no solid stems to stand on,
No hardened heart to help her.

We've all got causes:
Things we'll risk our lives for,
A price we'll sell our souls for.
Well, you just messed with mine -
She's my girl.

Wild cats and icicles,
Hugs and crosses.
Fun apart;
Fire together-
Feeding off each other.

Basics I

Puppy love
Check.
Heartbreak
Check.
Social humiliation
Check.

Next one,
Nice guy.

Basics II

First crushes
Crushed both of us girls;
Got to goodbye those boys -
Back to basics.

Tonight She's Going to Play I

She scurries in and slides across the booth.
She can't help being late everywhere she goes
Because every turn she takes
Leads her to another pretty face,
And she laughs, throwing back her hair.
When she's looking for company,
She swings out her legs and crosses them.
When she's looking for fun, she slips her shoes off
And kicks her legs up on the other chair.
The stereo blares, and she starts singing, dancing in her seat.
Then the boys come around.
They'll throw their little line, lean in, and smile.
She'll act coy and polite, enticing,
Like she's eating cotton candy
Or hiding a new tattoo under her shirt.
After all, she doesn't care if anybody's there -
She's just out to play.

Tonight She's Going to Play II

Bottle covered in frost mist
Numbing her underage fingertips,
Soft candlelight in her innocent eyes,
In her delicate ears sounds of Elvis alive.
Yeah, tonight she's a scavenger
For a Prada sport's suit
Or just a good pair of work boots.

What I See I

You remind me of
Bandanas and tattoos,
Motorcycles and leather,
Whiskey and steel guitars,
Dobermans and penthouses,
Red peppers and brawling crowds.
What's ahead of us now?

What I See II

When I look into your eyes
I see balloons and cake,
Swings and slides,
Baseball and bicycles,
Ladybugs and rainbows,
White onions and tunnels.
What do you see when you look in mine?

Shared I

Sharing lunches, rides, homework;
Combated cliques together -
Starting fights, spreading lies;
Shared first kisses -
You were there,
Pain of bitterness,
Haunted at seventeen.

Even when the air turns awkward and silent,
Over a first crush who berates and humiliates,
Best friends— always connected
We can fight or walk away;
But, we can't erase what we've been —
What remains erected
Because all the promises we made,
To stay — yes — best friends forever.

It's one of those days
That only a girl can understand.
Got hassled for missing breakfast
'Cause you were in a hurry to fail a test
And hear everyone gossip 'bout that kiss.
Nothing's gone right
Until he came into sight.
Now your grade and social standing in jeopardy
Doesn't matter half as much
As how many times he smiles at you,
Every word he chooses to say to you,
How long he ignores everyone else for you
And telling, reliving every detail
With your girl.

Found something we can't fully share…
Always love you more.

Shared II

I need sunrays
No more shades.
Our secret,
Our moment -
Promise to keep it
Just ours.
We joke truth; we cry lies.

Say Mine I

Yesterday we met;
Today you proclaimed:
Always your girl.
Is that a sign?
Should I run now?
Maniacal,
Irrational,
Or prophetic?
Simply a hopeless romantic?

Had a broken heart
You're mending it
Like a seamstress.

Anything I want…
Nothing's impossible;
Everything's magical
Long as it's quiet,
Coveted -
Our secret.

(Just have to get you
To kiss me again).

Watching,
Waiting,
Wanting more.

Say Mine II

You take my hand as though it's yours to have
And put it to my heart.
What am I to say to that?
You're the sweetest person I know.

You take your arms and wrap me inside,
Like I'm your best kept secret,
And so close our hearts beat together.
What am I to say to that?
You're the safest person I know.

You take my hair and brush it aside
And lay your head against my neck.
What am I to say to that?
You're the truest person I know.

You look at me like I was glowing
And gently kiss my lips.
What can I say to that?
You're my favorite person yet.

You showed up at my door and took me
Looking surprised as if unplanned.
What other knowledge eludes me?
And when are you going to kiss me again?

Dream-Delinquent I

He's gentle
Not in a rush
For anything
Concerning my heart.

He's funny
Just when everything overwhelms
To channel me to a parallel realm
For a brief bit.

He's protective
Like he's trying to shade
The sins of the world
From my sight.

Dream-Delinquent II

He's perceptive
Waiting for me
To stand
Before trying to steal my heart.

He's strong
Able to throw me over his shoulder
And carry me out of the party
Before returning to defend my honor.

He's patient
Waiting for my high to come down
Before putting me in place…
The only man handling me.

Rite of Passage I

Dresses,
Cramming teens in limousines like clowns,
Preoccupied with the after-party.
Guys need their wingmen;
Girls need their best friends.

Rite of Passage II

Used to be about
Bring It On
And *Mean Girls*
As we were coming out of middle school
By bashing the other girls' reputations.

Then, it was
Breakfast Club
And *Clueless*
As we were figuring out high school
By setting each other up.

Now, it's more like
Pretty in Pink
And *Footloose*
As we plan for the first night of our lives
By cutting loose,
Waiting for *Dirty Dancing* and *Pretty Woman*
And watching out for the *White Orchid*.

Caught in Arms I

There comes a day when the wind shifts harder
And the rain rushes in on blue skies:
Those are the days I want to rush to your arms.
Some nights the moon hides
And even one star won't let itself be found:
Those are the nights I want to hide in your arms.
There are moments in time that get stuck on replay
And memories eluding you in their games:
Those are the moments I want to be kept in your arms.

Butterflies swarming in my stomach,
Hesitation and anticipation weakening my body,
Can barely stand strong enough to walk,
And I can't write my name
When I see you've called.
In your arms can't feel the ground:
Wonder if it's there,
Don't really care
Don't want to come down.

Caught in Arms II

Never alone
But always isolated
Until you capture me.

Never secure
But always cowed
Until touch reassures me.

But the second you reach for my hand,
Or press your lips to mine,
I'm fine —
All reason left.

I am yours.

First Night I

Reckon you want me to wait
Save myself for you,
Give you everything of me
That can be just handed over…
Too easily.

What difference will it make
If it's only a few minutes in time?
What will it prove about me
If you end up leaving?

Butterfly flies past the ear;
Raindrop falls upon the lips;
Breeze brushes air across the neck;
Strand of wet hair falls on the shoulder;
Necklace swings against the chest;
Flower grazes past the arm;
Wave washes over the toes:
All in the moment
Of a first touch
Lasting through the wait
To touch me again.

First Night II

Confident
With your arm lain across the couch's back.
Hopeful
With you hand signaling come hither.
Soft
With your skin unscathed by age or sun.
Thankful
With your mind's awareness of a foolish girl's oversight.

A master of time
Heart over thought
Convincing
With your lips pressed against mine
In prayer no doubt.

He Calls Love   I

Jittery, elated,
Secure, enthralled,
Scared to death
On your way to him
Thinking it's right;
Thinking you love him.

He calls me…
Babe when he's had a hard day, and all he wants is a warm bed, a
    day off, and me;
Darling when he's feeling nostalgic;
Love when he's holding on to me like a trophy;
Sweetheart when he's carrying out the honey-do lists;
Pumpkin when we're babysitting the neighbor's little dickens;
Princess when my stubbornness makes him laugh.
Thinking it's meant to be;
Thinking he loves me.

He Calls Love II

Eager, clumsy,
Too easily triggered idolatry.
Impetuous, brazen,
Swearin' love.
Thinking it's right;
Thinking you love him.

He calls me…
Wildflower when I tell him he only has to make himself happy;
Sweetie when there's something on his mind that weighs down;
Sultry when he's completely filled with life and daydreams, too;
By name when he wants my attention, to let me know he knows I've
    done wrong;
Girl when he's trying to act cool, save face in front of the boys, like
    they don't know;
Woman when he's shocked at a burst of outgoingness or frustrated at
    a quirk;
But, my favorite is when he calls me baby 'cause that's when I know
    I'm his girl.
Thinking it's meant to be;
Thinking he loves me.

Just One I

One hug with our bodies engulfed in our arms,
One grasp of each other's hands,
One kiss slow and long - just one.

Laying on my back
Took in a deep breath
And let it out with a sigh.
Always my perfect one,
You whisper, "Sweet dreams,"
Before falling to sleep.

Where does the heart fall,
And who can ever predict
How into you mine fell -
A romance addict?

Laying my head to the side, start to cry;
At first can't grasp why
Then, in a breath of release,
I realize - I belong to you.

(And you're mine.)

Just One II

With your eyelids drawn
In a moment of exhaustion,
I want you to see me.

When your body aches to the bone
And you can't fix yourself or atone,
Feel me.

When your soul sinks
In lost dreams and forgotten purpose,
Remember me.

I know you don't need me,
But I need you to want me,
Make me yours alone.

One evening
One bottle
Found one love.

Signs I

Fortune tellers have their crystal balls;
The man on the moon has his caves;
The flowers have their daises;
The grass has its four-leaf clovers.
Seems everyone has a hand in -
Tricks in the cards.
All I have is this feeling and some hope.
I don't know what the future holds;
And, I can only wish and wait.

Signs II

You ask how I like her
For you.

I muster we'd still be
Best friends…
If not for you.

I know I loved you
In the fullness that came
When you were near.
I knew I loved her, my female counterpart,
The same way.
So, it painfully seems natural
That if you needed more than me,
She would be for you.

Shame on you for leaving
Without warning.
Shame on me for losing twice
Without seeing signs.

Breathless I

What did you say?
Forever and us?
Yours and Mine?
Wrapped in a question
But revealed in confirmation
Married?
Is that what you said?

Breathless II

Like hearing reindeer on the roof
Her eyes light up;
Like petting a rabbit
Her touch gentlest;
Like caught in the rain
Her smile becomes contagious;
Like standing in the moonlight
Her heart is delicate.
How her eyes dance before thee,
And her touch awakens thee.
How her smile infects thee,
And her heart invites thee.

(You chose her.)

Ms. Degree I

Could have gone
All the way -
The pull.
Now I'm glad
Chose to stay
Local.

Harvard on the Highway
Doesn't seem so bad
When I think about
Flowers on my car,
Him simply waiting
For his heart
Until I'm ready for the dream.

Ms. Degree II

Guess it's a good thing
I'm going away
Looks like I might need
That Ms. Degree.

NESTING

You shouldn't walk down an aisle
if an objection would change the direction.

Dinner Party I

On the balcony
Curled up with an afghan,
Glass of Chardonnay,
Wondering when the rest of life will begin.
Romantic. Breath-taking.

"What would you think
About us getting together
And staying together?"

"What would you think
Of being just mine?"

"What would you think
About waking up next to me every morning?"

Because that's what I've been thinking."

Dinner Party II

At a dinner party — wine and cheese,
I smiled and chatted and watched
Until I heard a voice — captivating.

You were never going to tell me?
Have you forgotten my existence?
Do you not even know I'm right here?

I went to find you when I returned;
I actually pulled the car right over
To be greeted with "Sorry darling, his job here is over."

I had nowhere else to look — except to her.
How could I call her and ask for you?
She adores me in my cloak of innocence
And elixir of friendship.

But, here, tonight I see I was right.
She was the only one who knew
Where to find you,
The one you proposed to.

I want to reach to you one last time.
But I fear, then, I'd be seeing your I Do's,
And I can't take another wedding
For my heart had love for you.

So good for you — she loves true;
I know - she loves me, too.
So take her, hold her, protect her -
Marry my best friend.
I'll learn to smile over tears.

Wedding Poem I

Most important day of my life —
Childhood over;
Commitment embraced;
Real life begun.

Maid of honor, a shadow —
Best friend? Adventuring;
Me? Left understanding:
Second best standing.

Photographer stills life —
For my reliving,
For your record.

Today I told the world I needed this man;
But, today, you were needed, too.

It's the season of love;
Forgiveness pours.

Wedding Poem II

Bet she's absolutely elated,
Picking out her life:
Jobs and houses
Names of little people and seating charts.

Bet you're all she's ever wanted —
Couldn't dream of more
Because I know her story.

I was standing next to her and her puppy love.
I was standing next to him when you swept in.
Heartbroken and devastated,
I was left to console.

I was standing next to you when you said you would undo the whole
     affair.
I was standing next to her when she cried love.
I was standing right there all the way.

But, when I finally stepped back,
You knelt down.
And now I'm standing all alone
In a nuptial shadow.

Celebrating your new life, toasting,
Stepped out onto the balcony,
Wondering if love will strike twice.
Spell-bound. Broken-hearted.

White Dress I

Sure I dressed in white frills
And rolled a baby carriage
With my child's godmother
At 5.

Sure I sat at picnic tables
And mapped out my wedding
With my maid of honor
At 11.

Sure I changed my name
And wrote it a thousand times
With heart-shaped dots
At 17.

Sure I stood in a church
And promised my life away
With my dearest groom
At 19.

White Dress II

Sure I carried your train
And kissed my heart away
With a "Congratulations"
In a dream too faint to avow.

I'm not sure I ever thought
You would actually leave.

I'm not sure I ever thought
I could feel depth without you.

You were going to be my dream-come-true:
Silver bells,
Red roses,
Soft candlelight,
Diamond ring.

How could you leave
When you were supposed to be
My white dress?

(I waited for you.)

Bessie I

Once in awhile
Jealousy consumes me
When I think about
The dreams we shared,
The paths we didn't
Between books and lectures,
Rings and fences,
Between dorms and adventures,
Bills and beds.

Then, I remember
Good for me,
At least one of us
Found love conventional,
And good for you,
At least one of us
Found life limitless.

Bessie II

Philosophy, history, art;
European tours;
Passion on the Palisades.

Languages, literature, theology, and ethology;
Foreign affairs;
Scholarship in abbeys and shrines.

Journalism, environmentalism, law;
Debates and interviews;
Wild in wilderness.

Anthropology, psychology, anatomy;
Labs and digs;
Tactile truth.

Physics, architecture, and all the rest;
European enchantments;
Latin liaisons;
Asian adventures;
Russian rendezvous;
American assimilation.

Invisible I

Sometimes I fancy myself invisible
When I find myself in comparison
To you -
The wild one,
Irresistible,
The hell-bent one,
Stunning.

I have my enduring eccentricities,
My favorable appearance,
My disciplined expertise,
My proclivity towards romance.

No,
I don't value myself in light of you;
But yes,
I see sometimes the world does.

Invisible II

Sitting there near your presence
I watched you from afar
Where I could see me running up to you
In a dream, like before, when we were free to be more
Than ex's and history, than past ghosts and memory.

I leaned down and
Whispered in your ear;
You glanced up eager and surprised to find
Me kissing you and pulling up a chair…

But here I am while you're over there
Bound by moral codes I can't bear to move
For if you see me, I must politely, but briefly, exchange pleasantries;
So, here I sit watching you, trying to be invisible,
While I miss you from afar.

And when the meal is over, I'll leave
With just a silent tear
That you won't see from there.

Allegiance I

The wind breezes by, tickling the plush flowers;
They drop their petals like tree limbs drop icicles
Who aren't strong enough or are just too wise
To hold onto that which needs to fly unencumbered
And just as the limbs bounce up in joy,
So do the stems dance with the air.
That's what love spurs;
That's why they say let go.
Sometimes you're so full of spirit,
You can't bear to tighten your hold,
So you let go and celebrate
Because you trust your heart to fate.

(So much for birds of a feather)

Allegiance II

Today
You question
My allegiance
As if
It's yours
To question.

That Girl I

Curious, innocent, smiling;
Mind and heart racing.
Blind faith leading;
Souls together.

Desperation, audaciousness, confidence;
Full disclosure as measurement
Of Love's sacrificial penance
Binding souls together.

Naïve, fool, infatuation, and passion fade subtle;
True loves dost make their hearts vulnerable
So easily targeted by others, too easily hurt by one another,
Breaking souls once together.

That Girl II

Watching you
Watch me
Was treacherous -
A land of mines.

Every smile
Watching how I held it;
Every word
Watching how I formed it;
Every glare
Watching if I'd break it.

Holding her
You asked about me.
Why am I that girl?
Are you okay?
Tap once for yes -
Piercing my silence
Had nothing to say -
Neither did she.

Waiting for me to rewind time,
Watching for me to fall from clouds,
Waiting for me to want you.
Perhaps it's best, I don't know
For what you were waiting.
But, why am I that girl?

Spent the Night I

Blessed
With the recent homecoming
Of the one with history,
Clocks now void of cacophony.

Spent the night waiting
For the college chronicle,
Intimate debacles —
Vicarious thrills.

Spent the night remembering
Childhood arcades,
Adolescent escapades,
First crush serenades,
Senior promenade,
Graduation accolades —
The glory that fades.

Spent the night realizing
Maturation,
Deepened affinity,
Everlasting loyalty.

Spent the Night II

Spent the night waiting
For you to reach your hand across
And graze mine,
For you to lean across
And kiss me,
For you to step closer in an embrace
And say, "I missed you."

Spent the night remembering
When I curled up in your arms
With my head upon your chest
Conversing endlessly, candidly, lovingly.

Spent the night realizing
There must have been a moment
Between "I'm not ready"
And "I've found someone else;"
But, we missed it.

Searching I

For the life of me
I can't find you
Because here's this phone
With its dial tone,
And numbers punched,
And silence on the other end.

There's so much space
Standing between us
That I can't find you.
Don't you know I need to?

Heart aches, eyes cry,
Dreams turned searches for you.

Why so distant?
Why not happier?
I got a fairy tale - this "ever after."

Searching II

Thought I was indelible
Blinded by invisible laws
Of sisterhood
And platonic relationships.

But I can't take it…
The glee in her gait,
The subconscious victory in her voice,
Happily-ever-after rejoicing in her heart…
You in her ballet arms.

The dream of us
Drowns me like raindrops on a cloud,
Batters me like leaves in the whip of the wind,
Teases me like babe bunny in the vegetable garden.

Nothing yet for not each other's,
But one day a power couple —
Fast car, casino, candlelight.

One day deferred.
Don't know how to take that
From her.

Behind Walls I

Making lists,
Checking tasks —
Honey-do.
Relax,
Bask —
Lovers' coup.
Gardening,
Cooking lessons -
Growing roots.
Boots under the bed;
Raindrops,
Lightning pops —
Baby says thank you.
And, maybe that would be enough,
If I could love like her — off the cuff.

Behind Walls II

You said I had that laugh,
My energetic laugh you called it.
You said you loved that laugh.

Ah, "love" the word we hide away
Behind walls,
The word we reserve, ration,
The word binding us in an Orient.

You asked why I was quiet;
I confessed I was nervous.
You assured me there was no reason,
But I knew there was — my secret, my love.
Are you blind or hiding
From the pangs
Of unfulfilled love?

You have so many imperfections
And there are so many reasons
That I shouldn't be so knotted up
With so little age shouldn't know how to be tied up.
Still, we exchange looks,
And we've learned how to make love
Through handshakes and hugs.
We're headed for such repercussions
For three hearts, three lives - running to put them all on the line.

My Closet I

Slip out of a cocktail dress
After Champaign toasts.
Step out of the black sling-backs
After dancing and dipping.
Slip off the diamonds and gold
After wining and dining.
Slip into lace and satin
For another night of touching heaven.
Spray on the Juice
For a vampire's bite.
Cut off the closet light
And turn on the night.

My Closet II

I sit here in the quiet, trying to escape from crowds,
In an old green t-shirt.
Somewhere in the hour, I'll start to look around at the past.
Time-traveling through…

The paths we did not take,
The ring I found after we professed our love,
The shoes I almost lost chasing after dreams,
The skirt that never let me down,
The award of childhood victories,
The photograph of us as King and Queen crowned,
The cologne that smells like the man I could have married,
The rose I found on my dashboard,
The note I found at heart's first bleed,
The passport stamped for life and love explored,
The teddy bear I refused to abandon,
The blanket that got passed around at the party,
The first homemade attempt I spun,
The book I read over and over to sleep.

Everything and everyone I ever loved
Left something behind for me to remember;
And, its home is here or
In this jade music box
She gave me.

(This is where I keep you.)

Dream I

Something's missing -
One more dream.
My destiny wasn't in ancient worlds
Or changing this modern one.
My destiny was with you:
Making a home, a life, a family.
Our relationship is strong, and our hearts open fields.
We've loved each other well.
Think we could find the same success
With a little lad or belle.
Let's grow our nest.

You, the parent —
Teaching and playing
While remaining pure and present;
Sharing lessons learned
Without needing to relive or justify;
Me, the woman -
Life's purpose realized, marriage cemented.

Dream II

There's a world
Outside of the suburbs.
It's baronial and miniscule.
Awe-inspiring and macabre,
Contemporary and passé.
But, it's also really cool,
Totally rocks…
Wish I could take
You both to that world.

He would fly;
She would hover.
He'd laugh;
She'd learn.

That Kind of Man I

He enjoys reading aloud to me -
Books, newspapers, even poetry.

He never forgets a holiday, birthday, or anniversary -
Ordering flowers or tickets to the ballet.

He showers me with gifts -
The Elvis stamp, the Chesapeake bracelet, and Tanzanite.

He makes me laugh even on the answering machine;
He makes me cry love reading letters.

That Kind of Man II

He's got a bottle popper
In the torn pocket
Of those tight Wranglers.
He's that kind of man.

He's got a jacked-up truck,
With a bed for a ten-point buck,
And stickers of Southern pride for luck.
He's that kind of man.

He's got rough hands,
An invincible stand,
And Twitty sounds.
He's that kind of man.

Yeah, he gets her done.
But, he's also the kind of man
That tends to be gone,
Doesn't know how to slow down,
Inadvertently loves his woman painfully
'Cause, though she's his eternity,
He just can't seem to let her be
His everything.

THIEVING

Just when you say perfection,
the pedestal will shake.
And, you can hold on,
but you can't escape fate.

Covert I

Nights out
At work
With the boys.

Covert   II

This feels wrong.
I want to see you,
But I can't get myself
To feel right inside
About reaching out to you tonight.

We all just need a friend
Because we've lost ourselves
And can't recognize the little one inside.
If I reach to you, I'll see her again -
You'll see her for me and put our hands together.

"Speak now or forever hold your peace;
Speak now if you need me,"
I heard you say on a Christmas past.
Speak now and save me, I felt.

Sonnet

Pulled over on the shoulder
Looking for a second chance in the fog.
With an anxious heart, I shiver,
And a mind racing through its files and logs.
Like a restless ghost a car sped in,
Nodded me and left with a breeze of risk.
Once stopped, anticipation overcame again.
Worried you were fading, I ran to you with a kiss.
I waited for you to unlock the door, fumbling.
You wanted me to wait — I waited, a mouse to fear;
You wanted the quiet — I screamed like rain in your ear;
You wanted to love me — I fell back into the cloudy mist.
You led me out with such a gentle hand and goodnight kiss;
I missed you before your driveway was out of sight.

***

Après ma petite mort
J'ai chassé un prêtre
Et j'ai confessé mon beau péché.

79

Whisper Love I

Wanting to crawl inside of you,
Descry the thoughts in your mind
That you try to hide,
Auscult to the calm
That I need -
Your heartbeat.

It's hard for me, too,
To keep trying,
Keep witnessing hope die,
Keep disappointing us
With little fruition to our love.

Not ready to release this seeming fate deplorable.
We're going to give each other the world.
But right now you're what I need.
To hear your heart whisper the love
That you don't always say.

Whisper Love II

So many
Have tried
To warm this heart
Of mine -
To impress with carnations,
To keep with diamonds.

One day I'll muster the strength
To tell you it's over.
But just as I start
You pull me close
And whisper love —
My curse.

Only Love I

As the sun sets
My lungs skip a breath
For I'm taken back by you
Standing in the doorway
You carried me through
With flowers in powder blue.

Only Love II

The only love I don't question in absence;
The only hand I reach for in the dark;
The only embrace I feel with eyes closed;
The only kiss I miss.

No steeple, rosary, priest
Can build boundaries
Between us;
But, she,
She does what God can't.

My faithfulness
You have in heart -
Perhaps you should have in part;
Yes, you have the word
I promised to her.

Entangled I

Your love confuses me.
Sometimes I don't know why…

So, I call you in the middle of the day
Looking to feel the spark,
But end up crying through excuses.

So, I reach for you
To find you asleep
And question the flicker in your eye.

Sometimes I don't know why,
If you're going to keep hiding
Some part of you away.
It's so hard to love that way-
Tangled up.

Entangled II

You were there behind a haze:
Can barely hear you;
Can barely see you;
And, I can't figure out
How to touch you,
Let alone save you.
Why can't you need me
For anything else,
Just once?

I wake up stomach in knots,
Covers mangled,
Still entangled
In your cries.

8 Years I

Is it just me or has something changed
'Cause things don't quite seem the same?
We started off with "Sleep sweet;"
Eight years later it's "Goodnight baby."
We started off with you singing to me;
Eight years later it's "Turn off the T.V."
Well, I just don't understand
'Cause you say you love me more now.
But, we started out with hours talking on the phone;
Now the only time you call is to ask, "When you comin' home?"

So here we go, let's toast to true love and eight years of us;
Can't wait to see how much more love can possibly love.
But you still say, "You're the one I miss;"
And you still ask, "How 'bout that kiss?"

8 Years Later II

Maybe I thought it would go away — this problem of mine;
If I turned my head, shut my mouth, and let affect go,
You would break her heart — instead of mine.

I miss
Your ghost stories,
Your warmth,
You hanging up on me, aggravated,
Your books,
Your drunk-happy dance,
Your ego,
You watching me sleep, patiently,
Your suede boots,
You tricking me, playfully,
Your big mug,
Your confidence,
You entertained by what would break my heart, light-footed,
Your vodka-lemonade kiss….

I miss so much of you
That every once in awhile I miss all of you,
And that's God's day.

Promise Easier I

I hear you promise me forever.
I feel you wrap me in your wings.
And, all I really know
Is don't let go;
I cannot lose you -
The words best friend and lover
Are wound too tightly together.
One more time, promise forever.

You remind me, gently, you've told me before.
You say I know more than I let myself believe —
No matter what we'll always be
Loving. Listening.

It makes me feel hazy,
Like I'm a few feet too many
Off the ground.
It makes me feel weak,
Like I'm two steps short of falling down.
Yet I still long for the sound
Of a promise forever.

(Go ahead, pulsate my heart.)

Promise Easier II

Only mistake was not loving enough;
The ashes of success are relationships.
So, hold someone else day-to-day,
And, once in awhile,
Insatiable,
I'll find my way to you -
Making commitment possible,
Making loss easier.

I won't fall
In your heart,
If someone else is there -
Keeping us the same,
Keeping love easier, if not fair.

Some Conversations I

A couple is meant to make love,
Redirect their lives unselfishly
To a bundle of unconditional love.
Today we're forced to believe
Our love will be enough.

(It's hard to breathe.)

Some Conversations II

Some conversations wait for you,
And some wait for a time,
Like shadows lurking on a walkway
Or mud puddles growing in rain.

This elephant has been looking at me
For eight years
Waiting to show itself to you.
My friends know your call by the bashful laughter in my voice,
Strangers on the street feel your presence by the glow in my cheeks,
And, she knows my love by my overflowing need to speak.

The elephant knows even more —
The deep fear young women hold in their bosom
As they suppress the motherly instinct.
We can't get but so close because I'm not ready for more.
Some men assume or would argue through A.,
And so the shadows and puddles get stepped in
And never cleaned up.
Tonight we slipped in the mud and landed on shadows.
If I landed in the predicament,
I wouldn't just fix it.

For sure I thought you would argue your case
Try and convince me that my convictions are wrong,
But you just stayed on with me in my moment,
My preemptive strike.
And when my words were done,
I heard you ask, "Would it be so bad, if you had my son?"
Then, I fell back
Into shock and said, "No,
I'm just not ready, ya know."
We held each other in silence
And watched our elephant fly away — smiling.

Body I

Found out this baby
Has the power to dash dreams.

Turns out the parts
That label me woman
Are not what they seem.

It hurts —
My own body
Hates me.

Do you?

***

He held me until I let go,
Kept stroking my shoulder,
Kissing my forehead.
He quietly waited for me to cry it out,
Letting me babble and chirp,
Until I passed out.
We woke still wrapped together,
Him assuring me
I was his only dream…
Beautiful…if only I could believe.
Then, I wondered
Why the one who flutters is fertile,
And my feminine nature is fickle.

Body II

The refusal I cannot make
Because of the heart too painful to break;
So, as a shadow of the strength I used to possess,
I continue as a ghost who cannot rest.

The truth I cannot behold
Because of the tie too important to fold;
So, as a child I entertain phantasms,
As I elevate falsehoods without reservations.

The affect I cannot tolerate
Because of the fear of challenging fate;
So, as a trickster, tears morph into laughter,
And as a poker champ, the signs I convince you to ignore.

Love Her I

Completely in your embrace -
Our hearts pounding against each other as I gasp for air,
My arms under yours, bending back, holding onto life jackets,
Our necks intertwined like llamas hugging to keep my head above water,
Lip synching without words.

Wish there was a little girl;
Love splatters.

Love Her II

Love her, so I can stop —
The lies. The betrayal.
Don't want to hurt her —
The one I loved like a sister.

Kept telling myself
This time…
Things will change.
But, here I am
At your door
Again,
Like you were at mine
A few nights ago.

So love her, so I can let go
Of the fantasy I carry
About you and I
With a quiet family life.

Love her, so you can forget me,
And she can breathe.

The Joining I

Today was another gray sky
Of heavy clouds and tears
Because I still don't know why....

So many become paper guardians
Making so many lock-key children
Neglected. Low priority.

Their innocence slipping away
Fast as this clock can tick.

The Joining II

Tomorrow will be showers
Of pansies and kisses.
But, I still don't know what love means.

To some — in love or redemption —
Marriage is the joining of souls,
And, the young lovers stay for years
On a honeymoon of life.

To others — the patient and planned —
Marriage is the union,
And, the business folks stay for years
In the boardroom.

You feel me uneasy
And reassure it's not cheating.
I admit two harsh truths —
It is: we just don't care.

Neither should be a sin,
Yet both seem to be
Through the lens of the other.

Need You I

Like trees need rain to grow roots,
Like the sun needs clouds to escape,
Like music needs dancers to take form,
Like religion needs followers to believe,
Every day we're apart is a day I need.

Trees don't thank the rain.
Clouds selfishly abstain.
Dancers' tired bodies disengage from the song.
Followers find a different path along the way.

But, every day you steal away
One truth reveals:
I need you.

Need You II

I'm not the girl
Anyone needs.

Fun like chasing a balloon;
Careless like a psychedelic;
Dangerous like the thorn of a rose.
So, I get why you need her.

But, the thing is
I need you.

Melt I

Tell me I'm crazy,
I'm out of my mind,
That I still get
Butterflies.

At the first sound of your voice, left smiling;
At the first kind word, twirling my hair;
At the first touch, floating;
At the first kiss, day-dreaming.
And, when you finally admit you want me forever —
You can't picture you're life without me,
You'd do anything to keep me -
I melt.

I don't need "I love you;"
I just want more of this.

Melt II

I run to you when I need a friend,
When I need to feel love again,
Running you down
Like a highway
Instead of a dream
Until I wake again.

But it's not enough for when we pull apart
Keep finding myself in a marathon start
Trying to find my way back
Even if it's the same old broken track.

I don't care; I may never learn.
I'm dodging branches in the forest forlorn
Waiting for your return
Or for this love to burn
Out.

Go ahead,
Throw water:
Help me melt.

Full Moon I

I feel guilty for wondering where you are,
As I picture you amidst the stacks afar.
I feel wrong for wondering where you are,
As I picture you still at work watching the clock.
I feel silly for wondering where you are,
As I picture you blaming other men and walking out.
I feel naïve for wondering where you are,
As I picture you in another's arms.

My emotions are a battlefield
Trying to fight each other off,
And so for my mere protection
I wonder where the hell you are.

Full Moon II

Full moon,
Porch swing,
Arm around,
Clinging,
Eye lock,
Soft desperation,
One question:

Were you with her?

Confident lie,
Gentle acceptance
We both know truth
Broken heart,
One in betrayal
One in deliverance,
Waiting for a shooting star.

Cat and Mouse I

Here you are being untrue;
I can tell when I'm being lied to,
Especially when by you.

I don't need to know where you are
Because I'm smart enough to know
There's a woman involved.
No need for branding.

Cat and Mouse II

Phone calls when she's away;
Ah, that mouse does play.

Should I fight for him?
Would there be any worth?
What good would a win be
If he really didn't love me?

Eyes closed - it gets dark, really dark,
Can't find my way out of my heart.
It's breaking, and it hurts;
And, I want to get away
From the shrills of disappointment
And the fray,
Unsure of the sin committed
But punished.

Lies and excuses;
Love and disappointment;
Hope and delusions.

To no conscious purpose did I harm, but he's livid.
The clocks won't let me spin back, so I'm left unable to correct
'Tis a dismal affect feeling utterly imperfect.

Nostalgic I

Arrive, apologize, appease, accept
My aching heart back to yours.

Call, confess, convince, coerce
My corpse back to your side.

Talk, trust, tamper, take
My thoughts back to your nous.

Clanging Champaign flutes,
Home movies on the set,
Legs across each other,
Arm around my neck.

Remembering when we first met:
First sang love songs,
First wrote vows,
Promising each other the world.

(Can you hear how strongly my heart beats?)

Nostalgic II

Ah, my dear old friend,
I remember that night, too,
When the drinks were hard
And the laughter free.

We pressed against each other,
So innocently,
Until it changed suddenly
Into possibility.

I walked away but didn't forget.
Years later on a sofa
With movies galore,
We found ourselves back like before.

I wasn't looking for anything
Besides what we were
Until you kissed me
Full embracing of me.

I walked away because fear;
I wasn't ready
To risk losing.

Fast forward to today,
And with a nostalgic sigh
We're left with the memory of
Innocence and possibility awry.

Stupid Girl I

The hours are running by
Long after the fall of the day sky,
But here I sit
Exhausted and awake.
Can't miss the chance to hear your voice
Or hear what words you might choose to say.

I'm a smart girl
Spent all night in a coffee shop
Reading philosophy.

But, I'm a stupid girl
Still awake
Waiting for anyone —
Even you.
Ah, but what else would I have myself do?

Stupid Girl II

"Stay?" - say she can wait.
Most days I share you
So well; so, give me today.

I miss you like bears miss berries,
Like hummingbirds miss honeysuckle,
Like nuns miss the church.
Hurry or find me in a moment weak;
Go ahead, take advantage.
Looked at me, deeply
Sighed my name with blame
Void of hope.
For a moment it sounded like
A resolve to love.

Almost everyone I know,
Including her,
Faulted me -
Don't reach out;
Don't ask for help;
Don't say what I need.
Here, now, I'm saying it to you.
(Never said it before.)
Here, now, how can you leave?
(Never say it again.)

Mourn I

Should I mourn and wail in tears?
Should I clothe in black garments and wait in retreat?
Should I light candles and beg for peace?
For I care not; I am bitter.
Resent burns within,
And solitude is your only safety
From my sin.

Whom am I to question love?
Whom am I to doubt vows made before God?

Mourn II

Wipe that tear before you come unglued
'Cause I can't take looking at you
With no hope, no grace, no gusto, lost face.
Everyone slides off track here and now.
You can go anywhere you want;
But, first, you've got to get up.
No need to stay on your knees head in your lap.
I don't know why you can't see — "This ain't what you need."

I used to look just for a night of fun,
But every time I did someone ended up in love.

Judgment Day I

Bricks and stones I cross
To hear the words
I say will never hurt me.

Judgment Day II

Waiting is just fine
When it's anything but
Your heart perched on the barbed line.

Two Options I

You're expiring;
I'm surreptitious now.
I'm sure that I need to be honest.

I'm not sure that I should;
I'm not sure that you won't hate me;
I'm not sure I won't lose.

You've got someone new;
There's no use in hiding.

Two Options II

You seem preoccupied
Suspicions of someone else on my mind.
Self-doubt is a foolish thing
'Cause any other man I have is without strings.

Yeah sure, so what
I make bad decisions
Like the rest of the world.

Confession
Brings only question
From you
In a voice of excitement.

You're right, I'm scared -
Feeling it right now.
I did more than let him go;
I told him to run to you.
Better than the truth.
Tell me it's a lie
That really you're ready to fight
About loyalty as you fly
To conclusions,
Or don't. What do I care?
You're the one with strings;
That's why you say hopeless, foolish things.

And I only see two options:
I 'fess up,
Or he gives up
One of us.

Plead for Reason I

Tell me she's remarkable
Altruistic, philanthropist,
Moral compass,
A regular doctor without borders.

Tell me she's special
Touches parts of your heart
You never knew existed
A regular match made in heaven.

Tell me she's everything
Could ever ask for
You're going to pledge yourself
In a regular church-and-cake kind of way.

Just tell me it's not
For boredom or regret,
Loneliness or poor judgment,
A regular cheap affair
You're destroying us.

Plead for Reason II

The phone rings or the clock clangs;
He rushes out -
You wonder where and whom.
I'm capturing his attention.
I know the serum would kill you,
So please don't ask:
If I'm the one,
Or how I could take a man
I knew was so taken by you.
I've found so many,
Superficial,
And so quickly they go
Without my heart to hold.
But our hunter went and found it
For me,
Our farmer went and watered it
For me,
Our locksmith went to protect it
For me.
We chose each other.
(Let me keep him.)

Three Times Regression I

Three times I reached out to you —
Three times you pulled away.
You're important
To my sanity:
It's hard to think straight without you.
To my body:
It's hard to breathe without you.
To my heart:
It's hard to heal without you.
So, three times I ask
Where you are?

Three Times Regression III

How many?
Why do you want me to have someone else?
Does it grab your attention?
Peak your interest?

I tell you the figures but make up relationships,
I tell you yes but make up the reasons,
I tell you anything to stop the questions -
I make things so easy for you.

Three times I lied — three times you asked
About a shadow so far in the past.
It was important,
So I restrained;
It would have crushed you,
So I refrained.
I couldn't remember the truth,
Even if you wanted me to -
Some memories we hid;
Others don't even stick inside.

If I tell you what she did to me,
It would mess you up;
If I tell you how care has shifted,
It would shock you;
If I tell you she is the cover that keeps our distance,
It would stop you.
And so easily I lie to hide
That which could hurt you
So easily.

Sheets Down I

What if I need you more?
Would you lay her sheets down
And come back to mine?

What if I cried in front of you
Like wily women do?

What if I begged on my knees
Make a desperate housewife's scene?

What if I could prove I need you, too
Like a cupid CSI?

Could we rewind?

Sheets Down II

You'll sneak out
Without waking me
To ease the cost of us
Because I know she still comes first.

Sometimes I wish
You hadn't given
So much of yourself away
On your big white day —
Left loving me
With what's left of the heart.

Because I'm here,
Reaching out across an empty bed,
Longing for that love,
Devastated each morning after.

Break-Catch I

Just break.
One two three…
I'm still waiting
For you to break me.
You're the only one
Turn me upside down;
Spin me round.
I look back in anticipation.
I'll stop, I'll jump out;
I'll run to you and get knocked down;
I want you to break me;
I'm waiting to fall.

Bang me up.
Knock me out
Of this nightmare.

Break-Catch II

How weak of a mind is mine
That every time my heart reminisces
I cave
To the longing that overtakes.
And suddenly,
I find
I require you again?

Could I love enough
To reach through
Rash rumors,
Haunted hours,
Suspicious space,
Desperate destinations
And catch you?

Need me
Something desperate,
Something breathless.

Insatiable Hunger

A woman's heart is a firing ground,
where no one is safe and peace is unfound.
A woman's wrath is when she has been failed
and failed herself,
when she has loved to no avail.

Lady Says Thank You I

Walked in
With sound
Unexpecting,
Routine.
Halted in the tracks
With a voice
In the bedroom.
I prayed it was next door.
As I shut my eyelids tight,
She sighed and moaned,
She laughed and moved.
I sank down in utter disbelief
Until I heard round two.
Laid my hands across my face
Trying to decide
What to do —
Cry, walk out, storm in, fight.
Heard a "thank you"
From your lady of the night.
You must have known
How you found the door ajar
And a handprint on
The bedroom window.

Lady Says Thank You II

You're alone;
I'm sad.
Showed up at two in the morn'.
Hadn't eaten days —
How I deal with pain.
You made eggs —
My paper crane.

***

Waking up to see
If you were still there,
Ensuring my mind doesn't deceive
At each hour into the clock I stare.

But, the first thing I saw
As my eyes opened
Was the outline
Of your body —
Softness, innocence of your skin.

And, the first thing I wanted to do
Was reach out and touch you —
I retract,
Buried back in Down.
You momentarily awake
Ask if I'm all right
Close my eyes, silent.
Can't say
Losing grasp on morality,
Blind-sighted to loyalty,
Tripping over emotions -
I'm losing my balance.

You're not mine to take.
How her I should thank
For this moment.

Breakdown I

Getting dressed,
Just threw something on,
Never looked in the mirror.

Driving out to lunch, got lost,
Broke down out of nowhere,
Crying, pecked my leg, screaming.

Desperate need for blood rush,
Coffee guy tried to make me smile,
Felt bad for him — smiled.

Made it through work,
On the couch, noise not T.V.,
Still working.

Phone call —
She asked why I was sad
Concluded it was overwork, overwhelmed
Lying in bed: tired, awake.

What if I was sad?
What if it was that night?
What if it was you?

God, I wish I knew
The secrets of the swan mute
Does it require death to finally, beautifully sing,
Or does the sailor of the Milky Way die quietly, without litany?

Breakdown II

Reaching out;
Look broken:
Sunken smile,
Trust withholding.

No peacocking,
No nesting,
Hibernating,
I suspect.

Gargantuan plays;
Deleterious relays.

All Week I

Here you are
Soft spoken, gentle embrace,
Asking what's wrong,
So concerned I'm hurt
Or something's going on.

Promising no need for secrets,
Begging for my trust,
My honesty.

Then, you say it:
Is it me? Not hardly.
Is it me and her: Not exactly.
It's us….
But that you don't say.

Mirage, Illusion, Lie
Because despite our truth,
No matter how deeply we love,
You were never mine,
You'll never be mine.

All Week II

Preoccupied —
Whose lies?

All week, all night, all morning
Spent waiting
For a call
Saying "See you soon."
Felt stood up.
No time for that.

Melancholic -
Which love makes you homesick?

All afternoon
Spent disappointment
In the one I couldn't' see -
Felt too little,
More genuine than ever.

Pensive —
Who must forgive?

All night
Spent restless
Saying "Sleep, bring him to me."
Reaching across the bed
Felt emptiness,
Might as well be 17 again.

Possessed —
Who's left?

Jolting Disgust I

Why the hell does one moment matter so much?
That's what you'd ask if I confronted you
You'd scoff get over it.

It's more than a moment —
Everything you know; your footing comes loose
Everything you felt, like safety, proved untrue.
It's not just a moment but the moment you lost it all.
Fell apart, forgot who you are.

And maybe if it was just a moment
Where you lost your heel, you would have moved on,
Hobbling, but still on your way.
Instead it's when you lost yourself and now everything's wrong.

Reality strikes with poisonous venom,
Pumping spoiled blood through the heart,
Warping veins.

Jolting Disgust II

I want to love you both:
You as my partner,
She as my sister.

But this moment
The sky's falling down,
And we're all going to drown.

You asked what it feels like
To know she witnessed
Me with her man.

I can't answer…
That jolting disgust again.

As much as I cherish
Every intimacy, every truth
Between us,
That moment is scarred
By your question,
Knowing how it must have destroyed her.

How could you ask about loving her?

Adrenaline I

I thought the only thing
That could dissever or char
Was that damn race car
That you cruised
Before I could even refuse.

You said you wouldn't lie.
Willing to pack inside
While I threw around ultimatums
You surely still can say verbatim.

I thought either you'd choose
To spend your nights late in a garage
Or go all in at a track.
Trading safety for adrenaline,
I thought that's how I'd lose you.

Silver with blue stripes
Like this white gold with sapphires.

Never thought you'd find that car another garage,
Never thought you'd then leave that car for another's arms,
Never thought it wasn't adrenaline but love lessened;
But, that's how you broke us.

Adrenaline II

I know she doesn't understand -
One start fires and one covers with sand.
I know all she really wants —
Wings and walls.

He's her little bit of danger;
I'm her fantasy novel.
We push to the brink;
She brings us back.
I tell him there's nothing he can't do,
"Tempt this life" -
He agrees; she cries.

Take Love I

Just like that
You take your love
Away.

I don't even know
How to love
That way.

People get locked
In my heart,
And fragments
Always survive.

With a few words
And no love
It's over.

I felt love from you
Before -
How can you just
Rip it
Out?

Take Love II

Things I wanted,
Now unsure,
Knowing what it is
To be yours.
Total belonging;
Quiet longing;
Straight to the point.

When a moment between us ends,
I close my eyes with tears
And just try to pretend…
Not missing, not empty
It's not because I want more
Than I'll let you give me
Or you're willing to do.
I just try to believe
This is how we…love.

Then, I disappear again
Like Persephone.

Sleeping Over I

Sleepovers and campsites:
We shared a bed
Like sisters.

How dare you
Share one with him.
What did you expect -
We would each lay our head
Upon his shoulder?

Sleeping Over II

I never told you,
Purposely hid from you -
Single secret.
Not because I couldn't face you;
But, the fear of losing you was insurmountable.
Now I know the colors of faith's feathers.

Now, the veil will show
How much of you
Is in the image of God.

Nightingale to Mockingbird I

Her name on your lips
Always commonplace,
A word we shared casually.

Lately the ring is piercing
As you attach hope and laughter
To these letters
In a way I never could.
In the way you used to say mine,
I hear her name.
And the hope for the friendship of my beloveds disappear,
And the peace of our intertwined existence,
And the laughter in our years left longing.
(Is nothing enough?)
Told me bad news
Should have listened to you.

I hear her name, and all I see
Is you — our bonds
Within this unnatural double helix.

I want to hear you
Call her
Yours — baby —
Whisper in my ear
What you tell her;
Run your hands across me like you do her;
Show me how you love her
Because I know how you love me.
Want to hear her pillow talk
Feel her arms around you
Feel her breathe shared serenity
Feel her love you

Because I know how I love you.
So you're better now
Because you have her.

Yes, say her name again,
So you can see
My skin pale
In sadness
And our love
Suicide.

Nightingale to Mockingbird II

Last night, while you were thinking
You didn't know what to do,
I was thinking,
I believe you —
Maybe in the end....

Last night was the first time
I laid next to a man
Not out of necessity for accommodations
And not because I needed to feel protected
But because I felt loved by him.

What am I supposed to do tomorrow
When I wake up without you?

Leaving Type I

Today, quiet,
Still for days
Want to be angry
To find you and yell,
"How dare you just leave?" -
Walk out on this diamond ring.
Then I think;
"Girl, don't care,"

If you're the leaving type,
You best get going,
No need for waiting
On a hurricane.
Why hang around knowing
You're waiting for an excuse?
If you're the leaving type,
Why am I surprised?
Always preferred the dangerous guy no ties,
Forgetting your path of goodbye.

Thought I knew you
We knew each other
Didn't see this coming,
And you didn't bother
To warn me, ease pain,
To spare me my heart.
I want to be distant and burst into sobs;
But, something inside knows you'll return —
Admitting wrongful action,
Expecting forgiveness —
Things you don't deserve,
If you're the leaving type.

So you best get going....

Leaving Type II

Choices come quick;
Consequences last forever.
Can't afford to fix
New mistakes.

Two does by a salt lick;
Hunter lain wait like a sniper -
Good shot.

Choices not chance
Is the consequence.
No mistake - clean shot.

Find Mine I

Here, packing
Procrastinating
Acclimating
Clandestine
Kinesthetic
Irreverent
Nostalgic
Gusto.

Walking away before the sale signs,
Swallowing the past,
Breathing you out.
God, I pray it's true
That I might not need you
Anymore
That I can walk away from love,
Broken and caustic,
To find something —
Mine.

Find Mine II

Given ownership
Given futurity
Yeah, people call it
The key to your heart.
Well you gave it away;
Not yours to command stay.
Penance and confessorship
To Mr. Confidence.

"If you're gonna be my girl
And only my girl…"

Words foreign
Meaning queasy
Because to me it means
Us.

This thing is real
So take me if you can
Go ahead and call yourself
My man.

The Surrender Box I

Left a box on your front porch
Filled with poetry books
We both highlighted,
Romance films
From lonely Saturday nights,
Jewelry and clothes
We traded like baseball cards.
I thought about trashing it all,
But couldn't.
Maybe you want it,
Or maybe this is all —
The scratch of a cue ball.

The Surrender Box II

Waited for you to bang down my door,
Break everything you ever gave me,
Listened for the screeching of "whore,"
Watched for my picture on the Judas tree,
Wanted to fight it out,
Have an all-out.

Instead all I got was a box,
And a car I can't bear to start.

Thought we had something to save,
Maybe we're just not that brave.

Bleeding Fog I

Longing to write to you
Yet without any words to speak
Because it hurts too deep.

It haunts me -
The placing of guilt and blame
Because it destroys all the words -
Replaced with raw nerve.

Longing to write
Left to bleed
Unable to leave
The fight.

Folded the blank letter
Under the polished ring
In the jewelry box.

What would I say?

How would we turn words into a fight?
When in the conversation would the wound
Between us break open and bleed?

I don't want any of that
Just want to feel close even in silence
To say something,
Something like miss you;
Wish I knew how to forgive you.

Bleeding Fog II

It's closing in like a coffin lid
As the fog rolls in, spirit-filled,
Laying still,
Nothing left
Alone and dark,
There's no light again.

Sure I knew him,
But lost you -
Not the fairy tale.

Never had someone hate me,
Wish misery upon me,
Banish me.

Never would have thought
It'd be you.

Made mistakes:
Ruined your white dress.
Just foolish, stupid notions -
"Forgive" as a possibility.

Fight Me I

Everybody's got to fight for something;
So, pick up your gloves
And fight for me.

I might walk away right now
Nothing stopping me today
So try —
Just try to make me stay.
Scream how I'm so short-sighted
Blame me for walking out too quickly
Beg me to remember how it first felt to love you
And fight me till I give in —

For one more day
Because another day could do the trick,
If you spent it fighting my heart
'Till I drowned in your guilt-ridden love and desperate promises.

Fight Me II

I don't know what you need,
So fight me.
Let me see who you are.
Kick and scream;
"I wanna watch you fall."

Let me know there's a place for me
Let me take you higher
Than you've ever been
Lift you up on a spiral wind.
I can wrap your dreams
In blankets of green
'Cause this is love and this is us,
If you let me.

Tell me what you need to feel safe in your skin
To feel whole inside again
'Cause we're not us,
If you're not there,
And I can't save you,
If you don't care.

This is where it can all come down —
All the love, all the dreams, all that we could be
If you don't fight and scream —
You still love me, you're still there,
This is us, come on we can bear it,
Kick the walls down, and move right through it
'Cause this is love and this is us:
Come on, baby, fall into me.

Admitting Mistakes I

Called tonight
Two weeks to the date
With that lonesome sound,
Admitting the mistakes
And the need for an ole friend in sights

Can't lose me;
Don't want to keep me
Like before.

Looking back there were people I should have held onto;
Should have seen their love and met it.
Then, they'd still be here today,
And I wouldn't be a bitch.

Looking back there were people I should have let go;
I should have seen their empty hearts
And I should have pushed them out of mine.
Then, I wouldn't be covered with scars today,
And I wouldn't be an impersonation of myself.

Admitting Mistakes II

I had you, and I let you go.
I loved you, and I refused to tell you.
I needed you, and I pushed you away.
I was more with you, and I hurt you.

Wish I could have saved you,
Wish I knew the words,
Wish I could have taught you
How to rule our world.

Words never did mean enough
Too weak to stand on their own;
They never meant a thing against all I did.

I hear you've fallen through
The abyss I once knew:
Ah, love and truth.

Forgive me, I still love you.
Come back to me, I still need you.

(Walk away from me; I'm the worst hurt for you.)

Silent Speaker I

Stone walls break;
Brackish waters toxify;
Icebergs cold as death start fires
In the heart.

Deception demystified;
Manipulation mollified.

Silent Speaker II

Stalking the phone, eavesdropping on rings
Unable to pick up, unable to speak.

Stomach tangled up in knots;
Lungs being sucked dry.

Forgotten how to fly;
Falling from the tree.

Flowers in Bloom I

The clouds are breaking as we speak
Across mountain ranges and majestic rivers.
The wind blows harder;
The rivers turn white.
Yet you try to speak.

People only talk about the one day
They lost their dreams.
Well, I've been through a few.
One day the flowers were in bloom;
But, all the life couldn't ease the longing.
One day it was thunderin' rain;
But, I could still hear my heart break.
One day the snow was piled up;
But, I could still see you were gone.

Nature will cover such noise
With its whistling, splashing, and thundering;
It will protect this heart
That has been true to its power.

Still a little broken
When flowers bloom,
Thunder sounds,
Snow falls,
And those days…
I feel alive; you seem dead —
Like a spirit lost, reaching out in desperation,
You are naïve.

Flowers in Bloom II

This is all I am
Without hiding, pretending;
No games.

Find closure,
Open your eyes,
And see just me.
Tell me what you need,
Then give me a chance
To be her here by your side.
Let me be more than the woman
With whom you breed.

Pieces of Us I

Breaking paper —
Your first love letter,
The apology after our first fight,
The note I still put in your briefcase.

Breaking wood —
Your fist through the wall,
The fireplace burning it all,
Every door in the house slammed.

Breaking metal —
The phone cord jerked from the wall,
The car keys missing from the basket,
The keyboard down the stairs.

Breaking lace —
The pillows pulled apart,
My wedding gown thrown out the window,
My purse waiting in the car.

Breaking crystal five years too soon—
Our wedding photo,
My Champaign glass,
The vase you used to fill with flowers.

Breaking gold, gold with no use —
Your birthday watch,
My Valentine's necklace,
Both our rings somewhere on the floor.

Breaking our entire life together
Into pieces of us.

Pieces of Us II

In the past
Long forgotten
Released,
So they say,
But who can forget…

The moment love first touched you,
The moment love first left you,
First betrayal,
First reconciliation,
First time you realized you're not the one
You thought you were
Or wanted to be?

The moment friendship left:
Spoiling, tainting, sinning love.
The moment you won
And realized
No victory.

Pieces of Us III

You do what you need to do
That's how I love you.
I'll stand here and take the punch,
I'll withstand being shunned,
I'll call defeat,
Anything to take the heat
From your better half -
Your Lylas.

Burned Hope I

Watched you
Blow out
The candle
Without reservation
Ample ambivalence.

I was devastated
You didn't even take my hand
To lead me out safely
Like you would have done
Before the brunette blonde.

Waited for a response,
An apology, farewell,
A declaration —
Hope.

Realized I was alone
After you turned
And walked
Wherever you went
Without me,
Doll face.

Burned Hope II

Turns out
Can't be friends
With a woman,
If you're sleeping
With her man.

Who knew? How sad.

At Least One I

Standing guard at my side
Following me around
Laying his head solemnly on my lap
Yes, here is his allegiance:
"He really likes you,"
She says in amazement
As we exchange custody
But I heard the jealousy.
I wanted to laugh;
I wanted to warn,
"You remember that."
At least one of our two males
Still needed me.

At Least One II

Certain questions are philosophical,
Overwhelmingly prophetic,
Like the proverbial falling tree.
Others are messier,
Disturbingly egotistical,
Like how much does he love me?

Well, I have at least one
That's foolish
And needy,
Overly greedy —
Could this really work
Like love for Lear.

Tears Tonight   I

No point in getting angry
Your fists or screams
Don't mean a thing.
Go ahead, anything that's left.
Why say what's harbored in your heart?
Why beg me to stay?
You can cry or apologize all you want
When you start to remember how it was before,
But don't shed a tear tonight…
Just let go.

Tears Tonight II

It's such a long way back to where we were okay —
In love, at peace, full of ourselves —
That sometimes the memories feel like a dream
That can't be separated into real and fiction.
If only the past was a boutique we could walk through,
Or theater we could watch for truth,
Or archeological dig so we could pull it back up,
Then we could know what was love
And what wasn't.
Maybe if we could know for sure,
You wouldn't hate me so much,
And I wouldn't miss you so deeply.

FLEDGE

Just 'cause you never thought you'd have to,
doesn't mean you can't live without her.

In the Forest I

Too much trust
Will turn you loose
In a wilderness
Deadly and entropic.

Sat in the forest
With a Bible to keep safe,
But I am not as strong as God.

In the next life
I will be you surely:
Misguided love
And traitor trust.

Don't face me again.
You have lost me; 'tis our end.

I am too broken to love,
Too suspicious to give second chances,
Too faithless to wait for fate.

In The Forest II

You may think it now
Not a temptress,
Not a heartless siren,
Nor a jezebel.

I didn't endeavor to be
The woman you couldn't be.
I didn't prey on you;
I just loved him.

Maybe one day you'll see
I'm not the devil in disguise

(While I'm still alive.)

Condition of My Heart I

Crystals in my eyes;
Kaleidoscopes in my mind.

Best friend —
Could reach right in
And feel my heart adorn
Predict its fragile flaw.

Baited line
Turns up empty;
Fish on the line
Makes a run
Or gets caught
Two lines, two poles —
Once my biggest fear;
But, I bet losing me —
Now yours.

Still able to ignore
And can't decide whom to blame…

He made promises;
You knew the condition
Of my heart.

Condition of My Heart II

So quiet
Soon so far away
So many hormones,
Endorphins
Still couldn't amend.

He broke my heart;
We broke yours.

Confirmations I

I used to run to you
Stuck with you
With nowhere to go.
I used to run from you
When you wouldn't go.

Now I keep looking for you to come home,
Keep waiting to hear you ring that phone.
All I get is silence, confirmations
That you are really gone.

I watched you leave
With tears you couldn't see
Telling myself I was wrong
To let you just move along.

What was I thinking
That led me to dreaming
I'd see you again,
It wasn't really the end?

What kind of fool did I become
While you were off having fun?

Confirmations II

Part of me wants to scream:
Ah, you perfect little prude
Turns out you lie after all
Because he talks.

Part of me wants to threaten:
You thought your little secrets were safe
But I have them now.

Part of me wants to confirm:
You thought he loved you more,
But he wouldn't break our vow.
He turned you down like nothin'
So much for your true lovin'.

But the largest part of me collects the truth
Like a bird preparing its winter nest:
You married young; I sowed oats -
Learned the same lesson…
Levity, omens
Vice, envy…
Both froze to death.

Ballooning I

When did our life together break apart?
When did our heart first begin to bleed?
When did our dreams drift away?

Not asking you to stay;
In fact I couldn't take that today
Not after I saw her in the bookstore
Blind-sighted: an image I can't ignore.

Just need to know when did love recede
Because between worlds in time I'm caught.
Only truth can bring me back,
Bring absolution.
Not looking for reconciliation
Too nested in
Despair and hatred
Just the time that love retracted —
That's all I'm asking.

***

You let go.
I'm drifting away.
It's over….

Ballooning II

Waiting
In mixed company
For time
Just for us -
An hour,
An afternoon,
A quick exchange
In the hallway.

Every doorbell,
Every car horn
Could be you
In my fantasy world.
Waiting…
Rings aren't enough.

(Take my breath away.)

At My Door I

Eleven days
One desire
One refuge

Eleven days
Heart caught
On barbed wire
No word from you

Eleven days
Debating- pick up the phone
Eleven days
Begging — put down the keys

Eleven days
Why try?
Eleven days
Passed goodbye.

At My Door II

Here you are on my doorstep, and I can't imagine why.
You left things between us so clear and definite,
What else could you possibly have to say?
So, I fumble with the door and ask,
"Are you gonna stay?"
You walk right in,
And I reckon that's an answer — bent.

Locked Away   I

Two stood for us as one
Two years ago.

Unplug my phone — silent rings
Close the curtain so faces disappear

Twisted love hath left us here
To find new aches within.

Lock myself away
Because I'm frozen,
Catatonic without you.
Truth asunder;
Tears fall leaving eyes as empty wells;
Falling in love a sign of weakness;
Fallen love equally a fault.

Two now, no longer one,
We separate
To stand for us apart.

Fade like a stain,
Wane like the moon,
Retract, disappear, do something soon.
I don't care nor need you —
Choking words — can't say it.
When I can't look at you,
Or be near you,
Or forgive you.

(So what if I was destroyed by you.)

Locked Away II

Let's escape,
Lock ourselves away
From prying eyes
And second guesses
Least for today.

Don't want a return
Even for a night
Locked away from the rest of your commitments
To the wife we captured.

Plans I

Had ideas,
Dreams,
Goals -
All wicked fantasies.

Prince Charming,
White dress,
Picket fence,
2.5 -
In that order.

Nine-to-five weekdays,
Evenings filled with adventure walks and mystery rides,
Monthly date nights and neighborhood game nights,
Saturday birthday parties and races,
Church on Sundays.

(Not the only one with plans.)

Plans II

Cash,
Space,
Time
We're running low
Despite best laid plans.

EPTs,
HCGs,
GYNs
We got
On God's plan.

Not Just Us I

Sources say you're not alone;
From what I hear, you've got a little one.
I can't decide what to think…

You'd be a great dad and deserve the chance;
But, I don't want us to lose our loving hands.

The girls we used to know
Smile and laugh, "Can you believe it?"
And wait to finally hear my statement.
They want to know I love you;
They want to know I'm jealous;
They want to know I don't know you
'Cause they get jealous.

All I know is I'm not ready for change,
So keep your news out of my range.
I like our talks just the way they are:
Full of "I miss you" and singing to the guitar.
We have everyone else to be responsible with;
We have all day long of giving our time away.
So let's just stay how we are —
Just us.

Not Just Us II

As a candle burns it poses danger and titillation.
A naïve and weary fool moves close
Surely it will heat and wound and scar.
But, the persistent and curious press further,
Moving far into the blue of the flame,
Where it's safe from the pain.

At the center of the light is the calm of the storm
That will house you all the days past,
If you stay faithful.
If you stray, you may find the fire
As bright as that first sight
That you investigated.

Shoes I

They say let go,
But I don't have you
To release.
Years ago you brought me here,
Unsuspecting on bended knee.
You asked me to give you
Myself for eternity,
So I did.

Tonight came, and the sky turned solemn and gray.
Showered, dressed
Tried on five pairs of shoes
Then, there was the ring I wanted to wear -
The ring I couldn't compose myself to touch.
What if people asked — I had no reply.
I closed the drawer and tried on
Three more pairs of shoes.
Painted nails, painted face
Listening to Bon Jovi
Changing to heels.
I came here for the memory
Unable to make a new one.
Of course someone asked:
I shuffled words around my mouth.

Party of one was a lie -
I was there with you.
They must have thought it was
Endearing — smiling on my behalf
To the dolled up table for one.
But, if they knew,
I do not doubt they would chastise.
Divorce is death

Only to the heart.
And when dreams pass through you
To fill someone else's womb,
It's a silent hysterectomy.
And, it is after all our anniversary,
So, here, I may not celebrate
Rather I am observing.
Some days are holidays to the unknowing.

Shoes II

Always saw
Shoes not by function
But subliminal message.

Wedges
High heels
Sling-backs
Stilettos

Messages like
Can stand on my own
Dance with me tonight
Take me home
Hand me a drink
Want to be alone
Hope you have a ring
Sorry's such a small word

Yes, shoes can say
"I'm yours if you ask;"
"I'll walk all over you."

Been to fifteen shops
Tried on a hundred pairs
Where will I find
"This wasn't planned"
Before she locks us both out?

Shell I

You're not the man
I remember.
You're a shell of the man
I knew.
Is this you, love-surrendered?
Is this what you meant with eager "I do?"

Social butterfly turned recluse;
Happy clam turned jaded;
Daredevil turned destroyer.

Shell II

My shelter
From measured demeanor.
My abode
For an after-glow.
My domicile
From social trials.
You're now where I dwell,
My not-so-immaculate,
Not-so-delicate,
Shell.

Shh I

Shh, stop talking before you say too much.
And we find ourselves trapped under the words.
Shh, stop explaining before you dig yourself too deep
And we run out of lies to comfort each other with.
Shh, stop trying before you realize there's nothing left.
And we've burned down every memory we have.
Shh, stop lying before you sugar coat it more
And we begin to mesh it with the truth.
Shh, stop apologizing before you fade away
And we become fragments of ourselves.
Shh....

What's over was what was broke.
What's left is not much more.
I love you for whom you could never be again.
You love me for whom you wished I could be.
That's not enough.
Shh, stop running before you lose sight of yourself
And we ignore there's somewhere else we're supposed to be.
Shh...just leave.

Shh II

Shh, don't want to talk responsibility
And fight over whom she should hate more.
Shh, don't want to talk guilt
And blame each other for being human.
Shh, don't want to talk love
And pervert us to fit a box.
Shh, just want to fall asleep next to your body
And wake up to a whole day with you.
Shh.

Graceful Goodbye I

Maybe I thought long ago
We would gracefully let go,
If it came time to say goodbye
In either of our eyes.
Maybe I was just a child
Thinking love worked like that:
You'd pull it close
Just to let it go
For it'd always come bounding back.
Maybe I thought there was nothing
We couldn't weather
As long as we found our way back together.
Now, I'm sitting here with all the papers and boxes on the floor
Reaching for a tissue, thinking how I thought we'd be more
Than the screaming and the anger,
Than the blaming and the lies.
So much for our love-founded goodbye.

Graceful Goodbye II

You don't want to hear me say
Goodbye.
And, I sure as hell don't want to say it;
But, silence won't keep you here.
Guess when I imagined this?
We were swearing we'd never speak again
Because you found something else to do during my party;
We were holding out on a pair of shoes
Because we were stubborn, gave us something to do;
We were jealous and judgmental
Because we loved too much like blood.
It was never a graceful goodbye that I imagined,
But it never was…
Unforgivable.

Residual Commitment I

We were always an us;
I never saw the day we weren't.
I went to be by your side again.

But, tonight we weren't together.
We came in the same car;
You held my keys in your pocket;
I held your drink in my hand;
I scowled when you had a drag;
You moved a chair for me;
But, I was your filler
Little more than an old friend —
Not even.

I don't know how to be this
I don't know how to be with you
And not be us all the way through.
Sure we had a good run
Eight years of just us.
But, I don't know if I can be this.

The girls decided to look at their men,
But I could attest to none.
You were always mine;
I was always yours.
But, I'm not your wife,
And everybody knows it.
Everyone was looking for her,
When they looked past me
Unable to even remember
Who I used to be
To you.

Residual Commitment II

I wanted a little fun;
He wanted a commitment.
He won;
I resented it.

Shores of Savior I

The waves crashed,
And the blue cradled me
But would not let you reach me.

I watched you love her
From shores afar.
I could hear
My glass heart shatter
At the distance.

And weak from thirst
I longed
To take your hand
For strength,
To embrace
For solace,
To ask
For rescue.

Then the blue hushed me to sleep,
Let me drift on gentler waves.
I prayed,
Begging for acceptance.

I woke to comfort,
Knowing she needs you more,
And begging for release
To save you
From my heart purloined.

Shores of Savior II

Loved you from the beginning;
But for a long time,
Drowning in a birdbath,
So hard watching you both love.
And now here you are
Handing over my lifeline.

For Sale I

"For Sale" — words almost too unreal to pronounce;
Our habitat blasted by deception and gestation.

How could you? Oh, too easily I assume.
Did you think back? Perhaps the memories are too long past, insufficient
Is this the end? An era disappears of laughter and innocence
Will you ever drive by again and recount what was by any definition
    a home?
This is the last I'll ever know of you, isn't it?

You'll walk away
Leaving me to drive by and say,
"This was once a home"
Until everyone forgets you were even there.
And perhaps one day I can bear
To pass without seeing the past
Like a ghost or dream
Stalking me.

For Sale II

Most wonderful thing
In the world
This is our dream —
A home for us and our little girl.

Want to make a family bed,
Build a little swing set,
Paint the door red…
Want to do anything
To forget.

MIGRATION

With time you forget who left first,
who's to blame more,
and most of all, you forget how to come back
when you've released regrets.

One I

One year ago
We were a family:
Husband, wife, house, dog.

Sure we were angry,
And seldom used the word love,
But his and her towels still hung.
Sure we had moved into separate bedrooms,
And we seldom ate in the same room,
But the answering machine still echoed both our names.

One year ago
Words like "we" and "us" still existed,
Words that since turned into avoidance and lies.
Now we're a family no more.

What took years to build took only one to destroy
What does that say about love?
About us — what kind of people must we be?
Are we naïve for thinking we would make it?
Foolish for letting love make decisions?
Weak for letting go so easily?
Failures for failing ourselves and each other?

One II

One year ago
We were wild:
Indecisive married man and a foolish girl.

Sure we were in love,
Forbidden fruit.
One word brought you to me -
Wasn't trying to trap you,
Would have made it without you.
You just wouldn't walk away from our family
That makes me lucky.
Evil,
But lucky.

Grunge I

Dark clouds came -
You enjoyed the shade.

Rain fell hard -
You blessed it.

Thunder echoed -
You appreciated the noise.

Lightning struck -
You cringed.

Missed every warning;
Dismissed every caution;
Avoided every counsel.

Now you want to know
How you didn't see
Your life falling apart.

Was this all a trick
A joke unforgivably sick?
The signs play with you now
Appearing, then hiding -
Unstable, unsettled, unsure.

Grunge II

Here we are now
On a blacklist.
No one will come close
Afraid of what they'll know.
The truth seeps out;
I'm falling under -
Such a burden being a wonder
For the stifled minds,
Who have long since died
Deep inside.
They reach in and pull me closer.
Waiting for mercy, all they hear is thunder.
Waiting for solace, all they get is pain.

Stuck in Spirals I

Here we are again
Stuck in time
Between your world
And mine.

When your husband
Takes another like a wife,
It pushes you far
Out of his life.

But in my heart
There's a reservation
And a memory
Awaiting recreation

Once a year
When we revisit
Those moments
When our lives fit

As we reveal
To each other
All we remember
Just to reseal —

The wound
The affection
The present place
The misdirection.

Stuck in Spirals II

Don't know how
Supposed to
Feel.

Feel something
Don't know
What's real
Like a spiral of time
Through a nursery rhyme.

Canvas I

Family photograph
On canvas of red velvet
Without subject of success
Engraved with confidence
Forever family.

Ah, so nice to witness
The man's found love again
I on the other hand
Am still picking up your mess
The glass shattered on the tile
The fire out of kindling.

How can I bear to be
In another portrait?
Reminder of hope
Reinforces the failure.

Canvas II

In the quiet
Fear strikes.
Impressions,
Superstitions
Haunts you
Till you crash
Into the sin
Of self-indulgence,
Self-destruction.

That's what I see
Looking back at me
On red velvet.

Words I

Voice hoarse
And words worse
Than vexed values
Towering
Over our heads.

Look here, I bleed
From childhood wounds,
From childhood wounds.
No longer feel the fairy-tale loom
Like thunderclouds:
Taunting.

My heart leaving
In a sad, silent destiny
You're too distant to see.
Needing you to miss me:
Validation.

Words II

Compromise,
Illusion of action,
Grips,
Like hookah
In a clean body.

Youth in the eyes,
Illusion of accountability,
Tricks,
Like color dreams
To the blind.

And love,
Our greatest fall,
Illusion of commitment,
Weighs,
Like the moon's
Gravitational pull.

Explains a lot,
A lot about women.

Quiet Strength   I

You said his name to me;
Everyone is afraid to -
You actually said his name.
And, when the sound hit my ears,
I didn't flinch,
I didn't get nauseous,
I didn't cry,
I just kept breathing…
I actually kept going.

(Good to know)

Quiet Strength II

Love isn't perfect,
Showy, concrete,
Or steady.

Love needs memories,
Time,
And motivation.

She's our
Not-so-quiet
Strength.

Stepping Out of Love I

Each week passing my Whiskey Jack
Seems to step back
Further away from me
Into shadows and now obscurity.

All it would take is a single step forward
And I could see you again.
Though the possibility stands,
Hope has since fallen in.

For today I watched you
With a final step
Disappear.

Past the point
Of hope
Saviors flew south.
Waiting for life
On a ghostly plane
Flocks laughing
As they pass
Out of reach
Ambivalent.

Stepping Out of Love II

You had your days;
I turn to play.
Watch me wave
Sayonara.
We won't regenerate
But I will reincarnate

(Watch me.)

Sand I

Haunted by every memory,
Our entire existence.
Resistance arrives too late
To slay a dragon,
Who has blown fire
Into your heart
Until it dissolves
Into blood.

A red river flows
Where love once shown,
And at each memory
That flashes by
The river breaks the dam,
Pouring doubt
Over bags of sand.

Sand II

Serenaded by impossible realities,
Taken possession of,
Through love,
Lied to.
At least not twice
As you do.

Push away once,
I back off;
Push away twice,
I'm already gone.

Never been one to live in sand castles,
But, here in our own malformed, fragile fairy tale,
Here until our sand runs out.

Dragging I

Finally, I see
This is how it was supposed to be;
Maybe I was your lily-white angel.
I thought you hurt me;
Maybe you saved me.

I can't hate you anymore.
I crossed a line.
Can't go back
Right or wrong.

I just know
Can't keep dragging you around.

Dragging II

Can't get back
Things lost
Or given away
Or things taken
Have you forgotten?
It's all the same
'Cause they aren't coming back again.

Hold on,
Beg,
Retrace every step.
But you're still without
With no one else to blame
But yourself.

Sunset   I

It's silent.
It's quiet.
It's still.
It's surreal.
And I'm sitting here
Breathing in…
Daydreams and wishful thinking
Memories and recreating
This just can't be the only way
To keep you.

Sunset II

We've been together
All of these years.
Guess I always figured…
Once,
Sometime in my lifetime.
Never thought
It'd keep happening.

But, we knew each other
For so long
I just knew it'd all end up okay.

I don't think she knows that.

Shattering Truth I

Listening to the answering machine
Waiting to hear your voice.
But, it wasn't there
At first.

Instead I heard the sound of my heart breaking
Ever so gently
With an infant's cry.

And suddenly all I heard
And suspected
And feared
Shot into mind.
I didn't want to know; oh
How easy to keep the lie.
For fear of letting love die.
It's always been just us
And now someone new —
I wish I could just make do.

(It hurts to love you.)

Shattering Truth II

Fall asleep…wake up
To the light of suns and moons.
Head on your shoulders;
Your arm around me;
Hand over your heart;
Your hand holding mine.

And, I sigh,
You're my forever.
I whisper, "I love you"
Into your sleeping ear.
And, I start to cry —
My perfect morning.

Returned I

I'm not still waiting.
Still torn,
Not still bleeding.
If you returned…
Seeing you wouldn't be enough
To convince me
From reality unscathed;
Hearing you wouldn't be enough
To prove
Words exist outside of lies and goodbyes;
Feeling you wouldn't be enough
To trust this love
Again.

Foolish women interpret loneliness and lust as love;
Foolish women choose love over life.
If you returned, I'd refuse
To live at your side
At the cost of me.

Returned II

A few years go by
The little bundle now a toddler,
But the divide
Caused a twice-loved monsieur.
Between you and I
Burns,
Survives.

Days I

We all have days that matter -
A day when we remember our lives changing.
How is it wrong for me to venture out to remember
The day I first found love,
Which years later we made
The day I first vowed anything of meaning?

We each have our days
Today is one of mine.
No, they wouldn't understand
That though love may have vanished,
And your presence fades,
I'm still here,
Remembering me in love.
Ah, I imagine you forgetting this moment.
That in a day or two,
You realize there was something about today,
Or that you hold this memory in anger;
And, as I sit here sipping wine, enjoying antipasti
In candlelight and red drapes,
You sit at a bar toasting the waitress,
Listening to the guy to your left
Complain about life and love
And the one to your right
Tell of turning to the Lord
For the health of his son, who never goes to church.
I listen to a couple laugh at the last fifty years today.
See, I'm here with you.
You cheer to hell with women with your new buddies;
I cheer to fifty years with mine.

(Are you sweet enough?)

Days II

Bittersweet days
Like family holidays
Or stepping out on your own.
Today I lost her
Years ago.
For love, yes,
But painful nonetheless.

Wild Horses I

I never ran like the hoses do on the island
Brave-heart and carefree.
I never jumped in like the dolphins playing in the wake
Laughing and riant.
I never spread my wings like seagulls against the wind
Heart-set and unbroken.

I never owned me
Couldn't see it's my legs, my body, my arms, my heart
Couldn't understand I could have run, dived, flown
To catch up to you as you were fading into the fog.
I let you go
Because I didn't know
Me.

Wild Horses II

Three of us
Were musketeers
Happy idealists, daydreamers.

Three of us
Are battered
By life, time, and each other.

How did we get to the point
Of divorce,
Of love outsourced,
Of pregnancy unplanned,
Of anti-depressants,
Of numbness?
Yes, how?

We were friends, family.
Now you're a drama queen,
I'm the bitch,
And he's poison to us both.

Where You Are I

I don't feel you there anymore.
Stopped reaching across the bed,
Stopped carrying the phone around,
Stopped seeing your car out of the corner of my eye,
Stopped looking for you amongst the faces,
Stopped playing our song,
Stopped replaying, analyzing every moment with you.
Just stopped loving you.

Pastimes pass
Favorite songs shift
The outfit that never let you down finally does
Happily ever after happens to never again
And the ache of the heart that accentuated passion and need
Now means a valve leaking,
And you favor sleep over sex or food.

This is where you are.
Just a few years older…
Social life colder,
Drinks poured stronger,
Work emergency busier,
Internal clock ticks faster.

The when and how eludes me;
The solutions disinterest me -
I just don't care;
I don't want you back there.
Now if people could just stop asking.

Where You Are II

Swore you'd never hurt her,
Swore you'd never make him choose,
Swore you'd have a family.
Never thought it'd mean you lose
Everything except the one whom you
Cherish, hold, instill, love, and devote.
This is supposed to be enough.

Look Around I

So far,
So good
Maybe I can stand
On my own.

Sometimes brought back to you
Because a lonely heart or senseless mind
But then I take a look around
And see I'm all right
I didn't curl up and die
No mental breakdown
Or psychotic abyss.

Look Around II

Held on for hours,
Awake through the night.
You may call this coward,
Still seems right.

Everywhere I turn -
Mobiles, teddy bears,
Noise-makers, plush blankets
All I know is
This ain't me.

Back to Love I

Where is love after the wrong path?
I need to find my way back,
So grab my hand and lead me.
I've felt it rest assure;
I've been full like that before.

You're not my first;
But, that ring has been tossed.

Back to Love II

I found my way back
To truth, to love,
To something totally real.

But, part of love
Is knowing, unselfishly.

This might not be
My path;
But right now
It's my favorite
Part of life,
Part of myself.
Part of us,
Part of this mess.

She needs me right now
Like I need her — crooked countdown.
And, when the time comes,
I'll know
Because I know
It's coming.

(She's my sand.)

Curious Man I

Glazed over your importance,
Omitted your existence
In a brief moment
With a curious man.
I wasn't lying to him;
I was denying you.
A friend, a partner, a lover —
You seem none of those
These days
You're a shadow of the man.
Naturally, quickly, irrevocably- sadly enough —
Your name never crossed my tongue,
And my gentleman caller
Never asked about shadows.

Curious Man II

Find it curious
You ever crossed the line:
Loved two at one time.
But I'd be foolish
To think we're not on borrowed time.

Kiss me,
Thank me,
Cherish me,
Love me,
So one day
You can leave me
In good conscience,
When you're ready.

Sensitive I

Learning
To reach
For a new touch
To not turn away
From a magic kiss
To relax
In a suitor's embrace
To let the heart race
In a hard-to-get chase
To let eyes linger
In an amorous glare
To catch a solace
In a friend's voice
To hold on tighter
At the night's end

Learning to love
Again.

Sensitive II

If I loved you all more today,
More tomorrow,
Would I become
The sensitive one?

Could my daughter have a better mother?
Could my sister have another bird-catcher?
Could my husband have a truer lover?

Belonged I

Last night someone asked me if
I belonged to him
My eyes welled up a bit
As I realized I no longer
Belonged to you.
Squeezed the pillow and bit my tongue
Don't know if I'm his yet
Knowing I'm not yours
Again I swirled words within
My mouth only gingerly slipping out
One at a time
Until something intelligible
Uttered its way out to his ears
Supportive, soothing, hopeful
He was satisfied
I moved through surprise to resolved.

Belonged II

Seeing the child
Perfect.
Knowing the child
Innocent.
Hearing the child
Blessed.
Knowing the child
Belongs to us.

I am still.

Questions I

They asked about you, "Did you ever marry…?"
And "no" just flew out of my mouth.
So easy to say?
Should have said "yes" and stayed by the book
Or, at least, paused in remembrance.
But all of our love got was "no."
It rolled out of my mouth so smoothly —
Never even paused;
And now, I can't help but wonder
Was that all we are.
Nothing.

I know we've been over,
Perhaps even sinned and regretful.
But I always assumed we were
More than suspension of disbelief.

Parents at heart;
Lovers in waiting;
Partners for life.

(I can hear you laughing.)

Questions II

Sometimes people do the math.
One day this little one's going to learn counting,
Days of the month,
How babies are born.
One day my own blood's gonna have questions, too.
What's she gonna think then?
What am I gonna say?

Locked Within I

Tonight I adventured as one would celebrate a Friday arrival.
On the way out, a perfectly familiar, long seen face appeared.
He hugged me, and I hugged back.
There was a pause for genuineness and sincerity.
It's been three years since you've been out.
You were off the map, yet down the street.
Your daughter is six.
I watched her play the other day.
A tear sucked in my eye as we parted
Though I did not cry.
When lovers part, friends must side.
I never could have faulted you.
But yet I see somehow I've missed you.
Memories are locked within people.
You unlocked a few.
For that I thank you.

Locked Within II

So, here I am
Locked within
Expectations of yours,
Dreams of mine.

For years we were friends
With a love no deeper.
I never meant to love you,
In fact perhaps I worked more
To achieve the contrary
In those years you were building a home.

Then, the expectations
And the dreams
Got the best of me.
It's a regret
I don't have;
But, it's a love
I lost.

Fearing your wrath,
Fearing your words,
Fearing your love past.
Still at an impasse.

Relinquished Love I

Maybe we were meant for love, or
Perhaps we were never meant at all.
It is true our incidents make and shape us -
Owing you so much.
Then again, I could have been more -
For surely a heart intact can grow best
Owing you nothing.

My debt we'll never know;
My past will never settle.
How does one reckon a broken soul?
How does one reckon the eternal loss of a heart?
I no longer question purpose
Just as I've quit looking for signs
I've even let go of my grip
And begun to forget our memory.

Hoping one last reassurance could emerge
That part of me you so unquestionably have
I hope you have taken care of it as I did -
For all those years before
I gave it away.

Relinquished Love II

Life holds so many roads
For us all to take
Follow one, find another, switch along the way.

But, this road -
Meant to be a commitment.
Everyone calls this my life.

Life holds so many possibilities
For us all to be
One truth.

I was never meant
To take this part of life
Away from you.
Never meant to be a mother
Except maybe to help you.

BROODING

Responsibility is a burden some farewell with and others nobly die under, doing the part as the soul falls apart. No one can advise you on what matters most, only manage a wrong or two until you find your truth.

On the Feet of God I

Escaped to the movies
A dark theater,
Where no one could see me,
Where I wasn't alone -
Stepped out for a moment.

On my way back
Found you before me
Like the moment the captain says
The ship's going down
Standing in shock
Then paddling to shore in panic.

That was me before you.
You said, "Hello" and asked how I was,
Then I almost lost my balance

When you asked about the details
Couldn't tell if you cared
Because either you were merely exchanging pleasantries
Or you couldn't hear me over the beat of your heart

Walked back to my seat
On the feet of God
Because I couldn't move mine —
Never was the leaving kind.

(When will I see you again?)

On the Feet of God II

Somewhere in the reprise
Sin shifted
Like a summer breeze -
I felt it.

How can you regret
What you knew as due
To settle the debt?

You could be
A day and a wake-up away
From a whisper song.

On the Feet of God III

I knew it was you when you walked in;
Somehow time kept our little sin.
Walking by I start to smell that fragrance you wear —
Temptation - in the air.

You were the last person
I thought I'd see here.
But you're the first face
To light my heart back up.
And you're the first taste
Of life.

Then you start to dance
Listen to your heels hit the floor
As I watch your skirt twirl
Hopin' for another chance.

Then you start to sing
It brings
Back everything
Like us on the wharf
Always holding on,
Like us on the porch
Lovin' through dawn,
Like us at the theater
Reunited by fate and popcorn.

Demanding from Me I

You want things from me
I don't know how to give;
You beg for my heart
And demand my strength
To let you in;
You command we've changed
In a tone of accusation and confidence.
I jump to defend my lies
And declare we have not.

It makes you laugh,
My sudden aptitude for certainty;
I now ponder whether you were laughing at
My naivety or willingness to lie, found out
And I wonder how much it even matters
We have become what we will
With or without our knowledge or approval of it.
A pain and joy of affection
Ah, Jack, the laugh does matter
For its affect caused with me lost
Callin' the nervous girl inside.
Some hearts take time to see and speak.

Demanding from Me II

I don't want to lose you,
And I don't want to hurt you;
But, I don't want to do this anymore.

Loving Man I

If a loving man
Had warned me,
"I hope he doesn't hurt your heart,"
I would have run
From him.

If a loving man
Had asked,
"Why him?"
I would have answered foolish but real
"He's the one I love."

And if that loving man
Returned to mend the pieces of me,
I wouldn't have let him:
I'm not you.

Now let that loving man
Ask me, "What did he do to deserve you?"
I'd have to say,
"I don't know;
But, I think he's got me."

Loving Man II

Tonight
You called me
Only to call her
Somewhere in the conversation
"My wife."
It felt like the room went dark,
Like I was in a balloon with the air sucked out,
Like the machine went red-line,
And slowly the tears ran across the phone
During the silence
You couldn't hear.

I have heard you say
Similar words
Before
You've even spoke of her
As your girl,
Your woman,
Simply yours,
But not by such a name.
But hearing your declaration tonight
Destroyed some piece of my inside.

It took everything
To not throw up.

The Girl in My Eyes I-II

Wanting to make you proud
Wanting to make a stand
Wanting for you to notice
Wanting for you to want me back.

Knowing our love was never enough
Knowing you've long since put me on a shelf in your mind
Knowing we're not twelve miles apart, but nine years away from each other
Knowing we're not the same two people as yesterday.

Wishing that if we could come back together
All that's changed me would erase from my history
Wishing that if we could find a way back to each other,
I could feel inside like I did back then

Wishing to be the girl you saw in my eyes
Knowing you could help me see her again
Waiting for a second chance.

Blurred Flashes I

Nameless
Blurred face
Exists
In my memory
Of last night
Amongst the flashes —
Dancing skin to skin
Indiscriminant incidents
Of a parallel universe
Where time transverses
And boundaries transcend
I can do anything
Until white clarity
Illuminated the night sky,
Striking my core.

Blurred memories
Burned into my brain
Until I painted my nails red
And kissed her little forehead.

Blurred Flashes II

If you were to reach me, would you try to save me?
It's okay to say no; we've got demons of our own.
So hard fighting with a broken soul;
So easy running from the fear
That your whole world ain't real —
We're just floating out of meaning,
Just dancing with shadows,
We're just lying, tired of trying
To find ourselves and hold on.

See us all the way you saw
Before…mea culpa.
Take the best of me,
Then forgive me.

On Your Knees I

Asked why you ever pursued me
Years past it mattering;
You said you loved my voice
Let me hear yours.

Wanna see
You on your knees
And hear you scream
Begging please,
"Love me."
Yeah, that's what I think I need.

If the air turns quiet,
I'll still glide through
Because I already know
The emptiness of you
From my cocoon.

When you first met my
Bruised dawning heart,
You asked, "What do you need
That he's not giving you?"
I said candidly, humbly,
"I need someone to ask how my day was,
Wait for the response, and care about the answer."
You said that wasn't too much to ask for,
And you asked, "How was your day?"
All these years later,
And if someone were to ask,
I'd have the same to say.

But, if you start to coo,
I'll follow you
Again
Not because I am wan
But because the mark of Cain.

On Your Knees II

I'm going to push until you leave
'Cause at least one of us will know
I'm not what you need.

Whatever this is
I don't want to do it anymore.

You can try, fail to stop me.
I've gotten good with practice:
A sage of sadness,
A guru of game.

Some know how to make love
From a wayward glance or coincidence;
I know how to destroy it
With doubt and distance.

I want to hear your voice,
But I'm tired of being sad.

I want to see you,
But I'm tired of being angry.

You won't even know
Till there's nothing to save
Like a lone firefighter
In a forest aflame.

I want you;
But, I need to save me.

(Let her thank me.)

Fall Back I

We loved.
He said
It was real;
He said
It can be again;
He said
Like that's all it will take
To mend.

I'm over you.
I said,
I'm not that girl.
I said,
Like my soul
Doesn't reminiscence years
Anymore.

Sure people fall out of love
But let's fall back in -
Très again?

Fall Back II

The catacombs of friendship
Are a labyrinth of brutal remorse -
The devil has a pistol grip
Tighter than God's laissez-faire force,
And the totality of a lover's heart
Can't ameliorate the chill,
So, you tease apart
The devil and God's will.

Apologies have no more realistic substance
Than Gothic romance,
Full of its superstition and deception,
Its unforgiving foreshadowing,
Its terror, irreversible harm, and depraved charm.

Let me fall back now
To the pure heart I had
And give you a dowry
With our man.

Based and Built I

Maybe it doesn't matter
People got "kids"
So you went out,
Left me,
Had a baby
With her,
Didn't work,
Returned
To raise one with me.

Love isn't based on blood;
But, what's love built on hurt and regret?

Based and Built II

Towers built on gravesites,
Civilizations built on battlefields,
Religion based on unsettling mysteries,
Reunions based on bitter partings -

Yes, love and beauty and peace can be built on pain,
Perhaps deeper and more enduring than if built on anything else.

I loved you both,
You both loved me,
Now let's love her.

Touched I

You held me so tight; I wondered who was dying:
A thousand seconds rushed by in our embrace,
And it could have been a thousand paper cranes
Because I felt our feet lift from the ground when we let go.

It's been years since we've been this close,
We never lost touch, yet what we lost… touch.

I wanted to go out and play,
But I couldn't walk away;
Even when you swore to come along,
It just felt wrong.

I was afraid we'd get separated,
Afraid our voice would get hushed,
If we dared to explore the world's everyday rush.
So we talked — everything from cotton candy to tragedy again.

After these years, here we are friends still
Standing side by side on the balcony, laughing as the sun sets.

Touched II

Took the other half of you;
Traded you half of me.

Love that little girl
Like she was born of you.

Know me, your friend,
Your pair-bond.

In and Out I

Not the first
Another ghost
Holds the distinction.
And I knew
The very moment
I fell in love.

But though there's no doubt
My heart was stabbed
And shattered,
I cannot determine when
Maybe it broke away
In pieces over years
Like the water steals back the sand.

My friends say
My heart was captured twice,
But I cannot determine the exact moment
I was yours,
Though I know without a doubt
The moment my heart fell out
Again.

In and Out II

I won't say I went about it all wrong
'Cause I followed my heart,
Never stayed where I didn't feel I belonged.

Always tested the waters before jumping in,
Questioned the calm expecting the storm,
Pushed many away hard knowing the limits of strength,
Learned from my mistakes, dismissing the twice bitten.

Filled my sights with mementos
And took detailed notes, so I wouldn't forget,
Fall victim to a moment of déjà vu or nostalgia.

Protected myself with mirages,
And it all kept me safe;
I was never blind again.
I did what I had to do,
Knowing I hurt people, too.
Flying away again.

When You Realize I

Always thought it would be loud, deafening
That moment of realization -
The one.

It's a quiet moment
Something stops you,
Pulls you out of yourself
Shows you the exchange of looks
The gentle embraces
And everything that is
Genuine.
There wasn't noise
No distraction
Just us.
And love
Again.

You pulled me tight to your body
When you realized I was holding on.

When You Realize II

Don't need anything more:
No use for love;
Flowers die;
Lipstick kisses fade away;
Ink of love notes bleed and blur.

Go ahead and realize
I'll ever only be
Your child's mother.

(And, I'm the one who told you to love her.)

Comforter I

Space,
Mundane days,
Silence,
Time misplaced.

Sometimes I forget
How great
We are
At love and life.

Comforter II

Out of the closet onto the bed
I placed two comfort memories.
My fingers run along the seams,
And I start to cry.

The last time I was in your arms was here;
The first time I heard you say love was here.
The last time I held you was here;
The last time I sang lullabies was here.
Now all I have left of you is here.

So, I take a little chug
Of vodka lemonade
From the big mug
On my Bombay tray.

Absent Cause I

Standing before the frozen foods
I broke down -
Heart sank deep into my chest,
Breath drawing shallow,
And cheeks streaked with water.
Maybe it was because
This was the loneliest place here
Maybe because
I couldn't avoid my reflection,
Maybe because
There was a cold rain waiting outside.

Either way
Began to realize
Standing in the line
As I was forced
To empty my own basket
Item by item,
Barely surviving…
This isn't real.

I would ask you
If you thought
This was a mistake;
But, I know your answer.
I would tell you
I can't do this;
But, there's no one else
I want to do this with.

Sitting in the car
Waiting to see
Through the tears,
The rain,
I decided if you call tonight from the other side,
I won't answer;
But, when you ask me to see you tomorrow,
I'll show up,
If I can see through the tears,
The rain.
All for someone's gain.

Absent Cause II

You have now been gone
For as long as you even were in my life.
It took X years for me to love you
And equally it has taken X years for my heart to ache over your absence.

Every once in awhile
My heart catches me by surprise
And flashes our love before my eyes.

I have little place for you in my life,
So my heart will continue to hold your memory.
I have no right to even whisper of a dream
That you would write or call
To ease my soul with one admission —
You don't regret every moment we ever spent together.

Ah, but of course you can't.
One of those moments
Brought you back.

Empathy I

I guess I used to see it coming; I guess I used to know
One day you wouldn't look to me quite like before
And that day we have sadly seen…
I saw you laugh with me this afternoon
On an occasion of great sadness and grief,
We found our solace again.
I saw you lean against the very same railing
And lean into me.

Empathy II

Listening to your theme song
Years after we have parted
I saw part of you — brand new,
What you tried to convince me
Was there underneath.

It's too late — passed gone
Couldn't handle it again.

But, for a moment,
I found you
And pulled you in
With empathy.

Red

The last time I saw
A memory pass me
The only thing he said,
Was
"I always loved you
In red."

And I couldn't help but feel
Him steal away all those years
We went our separate ways.

I thought about what sound
Would awaken his heart
When I turned around
And take us to the start.

But I knew
There was no use
In reaching out,
Breaking vows.

So, I bowed my head in prayer
That he'd forever see me standing there
In red.

~The End~

Would you like to see your manuscript become a book?

If you are interested in becoming a PublishAmerica author, please submit your manuscript for possible publication to us at:

acquisitions@publishamerica.com

You may also mail in your manuscript to:

**PublishAmerica
PO Box 151
Frederick, MD 21705**

www.publishamerica.com

Breinigsville, PA USA
04 April 2011
259105BV00001B/247/P

9 781456 068578